THE GOOD NEWS
FOR RACISM

From Liberation to Reconciliation

Dr. Van B. Gayton

ACKNOWLEDGMENT

I would like to thank Ellen, my wife, for walking with me for over 49 years in the racially intense atmosphere of this Nation.

She has been such a source of comfort and strength. She is my best friend and cheerleader. Ellen has helped me with my editing and my grammar.

I would aslo like to acknowledge Tabetha, my first and only daughter. If it were not for her dilemma, her biracial status, I would have never done the research in the Scripture. My love for her inspired me to seek the proper theology on interracial relationships.

I thank God that because of her Ph.D. from Wayne State University, she pushed me in the editing of my book. I would rather speak than write.

Last of all I would like to thank all my friends, Black and White in the body of Christ, who have loved and respected my family and me no matter what our race.

Forever grateful,
Van B. Gayton, D Min
Reformed Theological Seminary

TABLE OF CONTENTS

It was the mid 1970's and I was filled with great indignation. My mentor in the gospel and dearest friend told me that the elders of the fellowship we belonged to had made an outrageous request of me. They wanted me to make a public statement explaining that God had blessed my ministry because I had repented for my interracial marriage. I was the only Black preacher in the fellowship; even my spiritual mentor was white. The elders were concerned about how interracial marriage would be perceived by the people, since I had become the most popular speaker in all the churches. They feared some of the congregants would see my life and consider interracial marriage as being sanctioned by God.

The elders' main teaching on race relations was that God does not endorse intertribal marriages. They interpreted this from the Scripture where God had established tribal boundaries for Israel. Therefore, they believed that different races should not mix with each other. This was pure, unadulterated separatism and suboptimal exegetical skills, to say the least. The problem is that they were not unique in their segregation beliefs and practices. At that time, our whole nation was struggling with the politics of separatism and segregation. Dr. Martin Luther King Jr. said, "We must face the sad fact that at eleven o'clock Sunday morning when we stand to sing 'In Christ There Is No East or West', we stand in the most segregated hour in America" (King 1968).

I had naively walked into my Christian experience assuming that all Christians had been delivered from racial prejudice since Jesus had come into their lives. However, this was not true. My wife and I had experienced this prejudice not only from White churches, but from Black churches as well. We were once invited to an all Black church in the state of New Jersey. When we arrived we were greeted with mixed reviews. Some of the members vocally detested the presence of my White wife. New

Jersey suffered great racial tension historically, and the consequences were evident in the Church. I was forced to address the issue before the congregation. Much to my bewilderment my presentation did not solve the issue, it only exacerbated it.

Because such racial prejudice was part of my introduction to Christianity in both the White and Black church in the seventies, I was quickly made aware of the great need for work to be done to remove the wall of separation in the Church. I knew of no teaching being given to educate or heal the rift between the racially divided churches, and so, I began my own journey. This journey has not led me down the easiest of roads, but it has been a most enlightening road, to say the least.

So, how do we begin to dissolve the wall of separation between the Black church and the White church? There has been, and continues to be, a seemingly impenetrable wall of separation between them in the United States of America. This wall of separation built from racism and prejudice, is what scholars believe to be the original sin of America. Because of racism within, the Church as a whole has lost its efficacious nature in dealing with racism and prejudice throughout American culture. Furthermore, there is hypocritical posturing within this problem. This great nation is called the United States, and its Constitution was supposedly written for *all* citizens to exist in harmony, as equals. However, we all know that it was written for the wealthy, educated, elite White men coming from Europe.

Racism has been the biggest scar on the reputation of America, and the Church in particular, to this day. The introduction of slavery to this nation was the opening of Pandora's box for our history. Although the European settlers were both deistic and theistic in their worldview, like all people, they lacked morals in some areas. The Church was divided concerning the issue of slavery; this in part, led to our Civil War. The influences of the secular racist philosophies of Charles Darwin, Georg Hegel, and Immanuel Kant (among others) were mixed with racially biased White Christian theology. This produced a Gospel that was preferential to Europeans because of the Eurocentric racist hermeneutic. This dialectical progression of Christianity and secularism arrived on the shores of America and was expressly practiced by the churches apart from the Quakers and Abolitionists. Many of the denominations were divided over this issue. The Southern states were more pro-slavery than the Northern states, primarily for economic reasons. This is not to suggest that the North was more righteous than the South. In fact, C. Eric Lincoln and Lawrence H. Mamiya wrote:

> The first separate denominations to be formed by African Americans in the United States were Methodist. The early black Methodist churches, conferences and denominations were organized by free black people in the North in response to stultifying and demeaning conditions attending membership in the white-controlled Methodist Episcopal churches (Lincoln and Mamiya 1990, 47).

My personal interest in the subject of racism in the Church is due in large part to being in a miscegenous relationship. At the inception of my marriage to my wife Ellen, we were both very naïve to the prior laws existing through the 1960s against mixed marriages. We were married in 1970, and the word went out among many White families in our town to not allow your White daughters to date Black men, or they may end up married to them. The birth of our daughter brought a new dimension into the equation. How do we help our daughter understand the prejudice in the Church and the biblical rationale for race relationships? In her teenage years, she began to question her identity and what she should do to resolve the inner struggle. To which world did she belong? We immediately went to the Scriptures to see what the Bible said on the issue of race. I searched many Eurocentric commentaries and authors to get their interpretations, only to find very prejudiced, condescending thoughts. Even the Jewish commentary showed racial prejudice; I will show the depth of this disposition later.

I repeatedly discovered the overwhelming prejudice and ignorance that scholars and clergy possessed on this issue. Inversely, Christians from both the Black and White church who were favorable to mixing of races, or at least not condemnatory, offered little or no theological support for their positions. It was more of an intuitive feeling, with only a few verses from Scripture for support. This lack of intellectual integrity is what led me on my academic journey to discover the truth on the subject. I was living between two Christian worlds but not totally accepted in either one, merely due to my marriage.

In search for truth, some Black scholars have developed a Black theology, liberal in their approach for the most part. They are academically aware of the racist card being played by White theologians. Thus, they do have a tendency to overemphasize the position of Blacks in God's creation of humanity instead of the equality of our existence among all ethnic groups. What we need is a Gospel that is universal and yet flavored with an Afrocentric hermeneutic at the same time.

America is at a crossroad. Diane Sawyer interviewed Billy Graham on *Prime Time Live*, asking him, "If you could wave your hand and make one problem in this world go away, what would that be?" Instantly, he responded "Racial division and strife" (R.C. Rosser, 1998).

W.E.B. Du Bois admonished America that the greatest problem facing America during the twentieth century would be "the problem of the color line" (Du Bois 2003, 3). This may be an underlying cause for the fall of another civilization. The United States of America, called by some a Christian nation, is failing to solve the historic problem of racism, thus contributing to the cause of continual bigotry. The Church has not heeded the words of our Savior to be salt and light. Jesus said in His high priestly prayer, *"that they may all be one [...] so that the world may believe that you have sent me"* (John 17:21). The hope is that the Black church and White church will heed the call of God and courageously step up to this challenge to bring true unity within our diversity. God is defined as "distinct but inseparable" and so should be the character of His church.

In today's climate, to have a rational conversation about race is almost impossible. It is emotionally uncomfortable for both Blacks and Whites. Blacks have to bare the pain and Whites have to bare the shame. The Church is another place where no one wants to talk about the problem of race, which exacerbates the issue. We are not comfortable having dialogue let alone discussing the theology of slavery and racism. You will notice not many pulpits, when exegeting a text, bring out the racial implications that are so clearly present. Why is this the case in the Church? How do we flip the script? How do we fix it?

A survey of the Old Testament and the New Testament will help ascertain God's disposition in creating a diverse humanity who come together for His glory. Scripture will demonstrate that it is a loving God's idea that all His children, no matter the ethnicity, are one. It will also reveal separatism due to fallen humanity under the influence of Satan, and the Gospel message presented as a redemptive plan that is inclusive of all ethnicity. Only the truth of the Gospel is able to tear down the walls of separation among us and bring healing, comfort and peace. We are called to be the salt of the earth and the light of the world, but if we do not talk about racial issues, we will never heal. Preaching the message of good news is the Church's best way to obey Christ and bring joy to the world. We are called to be the "carriers" of God's story, as well as "characters" in God's story.

One might ask, what is the good news in this story? *Gospel,* from the Greek, means good news. The ancient world picture was the idea of a king going off to battle against another king or kings. Now no one would know how the battle was going for some time, since there was no Internet. On the way back from a battle to his kingdom, a procession would form celebrating the king's victory with shouts of, "Our king won!" The Gospel is the story of Jesus going to battle on behalf of the kingdom of God against the kingdom of darkness—and winning. We announce the good news to all people that "Jesus reigns" overall.

Our Creator made us to love stories. We all love certain kinds of stories, but the story of God is the greatest story ever told. Concerning the Bible, many people begin reading in the middle of the story, or the New Testament. No one watches television or reads a book beginning in the middle or near the end. Most Christians' understanding of the Gospel is that Jesus lived, died, and rose again from the dead to save sinners. Although this is absolutely the truth, it is not the whole story. The Gospel is the good news of Jesus, from Genesis to Revelation.

God's story is called the metanarrative or story above all stories. This story can be simplified into four acts in the divine drama. Act one is the Creation, act two is the Fall of man and angels, act three is Redemption, and act four is the Consummation of all things. In this book, we will walk through all four acts of the divine drama. It is through these acts that we are able to answer the four philosophical questions of life: How/why are we here? What went wrong? How do we fix it? And, where do we go from here at death? Each of the acts will be elaborated on as they relate to racism and show how the good news is the only solution. The Gospel speaks to all of man's ills, including racism and prejudice, and has the power to deliver us.

The purpose of this book is to make sure that Christian America understands how to look at the Gospel story from a more Afrocentric hermeneutic position, emphasizing the verses that specifically highlight God's position on racial diversity. Secondly, to walk through the redemptive good news of the Gospel story that takes us from liberation to reconciliation unto Christ. It is the redemptive story that liberates us from the residual shackles of the past. It heals us from the psychological, emotional, intellectual, and socioeconomic bondage of the feeling of inferiority for Blacks and the sense of superiority for Whites, so that we can be reconciled as one, as equals. In the pursuit of reconciliation, the Church must: 1) understand and acknowledge racism and prejudice, 2) participate in a redemptive dialog towards reconciliation, and 3) implement a strategy with integrity to heal our nation.

CHAPTER ONE

DIVINE DRAMA ACT 1:
DOCTRINE OF CREATION

Why Are We Here?

The origin of the human race according to the Bible is found in the book of Genesis. The first act of Elohim is a six-day (*Yom* is the Hebrew term for day and can mean a 24-hour day or an extended period of time) creation, which is performed *ex nihilo*, meaning out of nothing. The first revelation of God is the Creator of the heavens and earth. The phrase, heavens and earth is used to convey the idea of the universe, because the Hebrew language has no word for universe.

The theological/philosophical phrase for God as Creator is transcendent causal agent. Transcendent means that God exists outside of space, matter, and time and is not subject to natural laws, but is the Creator of natural laws. He is a higher being, which is not meant to be understood in a geographical sense, but as higher in quality of being. This trait distinguishes God from all created things and requires Him to be personal and eternal, all-powerful and all-knowing, the uncreated Creator. Theologically and philosophically, the existence of all things requires that such a being exist, or there could be nothing at all.

It is a basic truism that something cannot come from nothing. The Genesis account answers the philosophical question: How did we get here? The Bible also provides a valid and reasonable explanation for the more important question: Why is there something instead of nothing? The universe cannot be self-created because this is an irrational and non-defensible proposition. Dr. R.C. Sproul teaches that there are only four perspectives about creation. First, creation is eternal. Although Aristotle taught this, that God used pre-existing matter as the material to make the universe, it has been proven untrue. By the second law of thermodynamics, called entropy, everything goes from order to chaos. Science has proven the universe is expanding and cooling off at the same time. It is coming to an end; therefore, it had to have a beginning. Second, creation is an illusion as taught in Eastern Mysticism, which denies thought behind the creation of this world and the reality of evil in this world. This is an irrational worldview since it is easy to look around and see that real evil does exist. Third, creation is the result of evolution, and is therefore self-created. How do you get something from nothing? Evolution theory presupposes that something existed, before it existed, in order to create itself. They try to validate this worldview by time and chance. But, no amount of time or chance can justify the illogical thought that something has the ability to create itself before it ever existed. Fourth, an eternal, personal, all-powerful, and all-knowing triune God created something out of nothing for His glory (Sproul, 2001). There was nothing, but God wanted something, and so he said, "Let there be…"

From a Gospel perspective, the book of Genesis conveys that a transcendent, yet immanent God created the universe and everything in it at the beginning of time. God is immanent because He can intervene into His creation at will, yet this is not a violation of natural law because He is the Creator of natural law. The Apostle's Creed states: "I believe in God, the Father almighty, maker of Heaven and Earth." The Nicene Creed adds: "maker of all things seen and unseen." The God of the Bible is repeatedly revealed as the uncreated Creator. Although He is distinct from His creation, He is not distant from it. All of this conveys the understanding that when God created humankind it was a sovereign, benevolent, and self-determined act of His will. Creation by a benevolent God is the only reasonable explanation for existence. God was not lonely with a triune existence, but by His generous nature gave us life.

In Genesis 1:26-27, *Then God said, "Let us make man in our image, after our likeness. And let them have dominion over the fish of the sea and over the birds of the heavens and over the livestock and over all the earth and over every creeping thing that creeps on the earth."*[27] *So God created man in his own image, in the image of God he created him; male and female he created them.* God seems to make some clear distinctions between humans and the rest of His creation. First, we notice until man the text says, "Let there be," but with humans He said, "Let us make man." So, Adam and Eve were created on the sixth day of creation. Secondly, all humans (and only humans) are created as the image of God, to be in personal relationship with Him and to reflect His glory. The significance of this truth is that God has a different kind of relationship with Adam and Eve than He does with the rest of His creation. They were the crowns of His creation and God said it was very good. Humans therefore represent God on the earth; it is a matter of function.

Philo of Alexandria originated the Latin term *Imago Dei* meaning image of God. He taught that our human reasoning was what made us in the image of God. Irenaeus was next and taught that it was our spirit that made us in the image of God. Finally, Thomas Aquinas taught free will was what made us in God's likeness. But it goes deeper than these human attributes. Humans are the *imagers of God*. The attributes help us to function as ambassadors of God. We could translate the verse to say "as" the image of God instead of "in" the image of God because "as" denotes function. We are the earthly representatives of Elohim. This function is further explained when God gives Adam a cultural mandate in Genesis 1:28, [...] *God said to them, "Be fruitful and multiply and fill the earth and subdue it, and have dominion over the fish of the sea and over the birds of the heavens and over every living thing that moves on the earth."* This is referred to as the dominion mandate. The whole human race as imagers of God was intended to rule over and be stewards of God's creation. So, the impression that the Genesis account gives is that God made everything for Himself primarily and for man secondarily. The universe, particularly planet earth, was specifically fashioned for human habitation. This unique design for human occupation is called the anthropic principle. All the laws of nature are constant for the sake of human existence. God is not only the Creator, but also the sustainer of the universe.

Additionally, Genesis 2:7 revealed, *"then the Lord God formed the man of dust from the ground and breathed into his nostrils the breath of life, and the man became a living creature."* No other form of creation was brought forth from the very breath of God, the primary source of human life, dignity and worth.

Creation and Racism

The Scriptures explicitly teach that the origin of humankind was God, who is indiscriminate and loves variety. He created Adam and then Eve from the ground and breathed into them. From Adam and Eve came all humans who followed. The very breath of God was given to humankind, in every ethnic group around the globe. Inherent within the creative act of God, there is equality among all ethnicities and both genders. Therefore, no human group should feel superior over any other human group. Unmistakably, equality is a God idea and all of God's ideas are very good. This is the essential nature of God our Creator to show no partiality (Acts 10:34).

The human race owes its existence to the God of the Scriptures (Genesis 1; John 1:1-4). The fact that we are made as His imagers means we are His offspring. If the God of the Bible is our Creator, then we have a basis of equality, since He did not give any delineation to our ethnic differences. We all have the same Creator and should look at each other equally as a God idea. This puts our relationships in perspective, as children all having the same Father. This also rules out the practice of dehumanization, which includes racism, slavery, prejudice and discrimination.

The good news is based on the character of God. So, it is *sine qua non* that He be revealed as loving, just, and impartial. The heart of the Father must always be perceived as loving all, whom He has created equally. The distinction of ethnicity is reflected in His triune nature. Father, Son, and Holy Spirit are distinct but inseparable, so we should recognize that God celebrates our diversity and is exalted in our inseparability.

It would be contrary to Scripture to think of God as favoring some of His children based on ethnicity alone. Throughout the Scriptures God has used people from the three sons of Noah to produce His good pleasure in the earth (Genesis 9). We have seen people from all three sons of Noah blessed and cursed due to their actions, not their inherent worth.

We are part of the expression of God in the earth. Our fellowship with Him is demonstrated in the dimensions of not only our emotions and rationale, but also the skill sets that He gave us. Our ability to reason and our imagination are also gifts from God. It should be noted that God did not give every human being the same measure of gifts and talents. This means that some people excel more than others in any given discipline. W.E.B. Du Bois (2003) calls this the talented tenth. These gifting differences should not be interpreted as some people being of greater worth or respect than others. The greater gift is indicative of greater responsibility. Although we are not all equipped the same, our differences cause us to need each other and interact with each other for the well-being of all, not for the purpose of discrimination. God's design produces interdependence, not independence. We all bring something to the table of humanity's function on earth.

It appears that God was not satisfied just to make us; He made humans with a *purpose*. The Genesis text gives the understanding that God's intent concerning the cultural mandate was for all humans. The perfect environment for all humans is to love and serve each other for the glory of God, the Father of us all. This understanding of the creation of the world, and humans in particular, must be the bedrock for any further discussion concerning the equality and dignity of all ethnicities. We share as His image and a finite display of His attributes, such as creativity and rule. He is distinct from us, but not distant from us. So, when God said [...] *"Be fruitful and multiply, take dominion [...]"* in Genesis 1:28, it was put in us to do so by our Creator's gifting.

In the Garden of Eden there is the implicit ideal of perfect harmony among humans and the rest of creation because of the absence of a fallen human nature. If there is no sinful nature, there cannot be any sinful dispositions. This is the utopia that humankind presently longs for in family, church, and society. The perfect environment was all of humanity exercising dominion over creation under God's sovereignty. Dominion is part of the concept of Paradise that God gave to Adam and Eve. However, it was apparent that God did not want us to dominate each other, He is an equal worth employer to all the descendants of Adam.

Nowhere in the creation narrative of Genesis do we find a hint of God's intent to discriminate or show partiality in human's ability to fulfill the cultural mandate. Nowhere in God's Word do we see Paradise consisting of capitalistic exploitation to the detriment of the rest of the population; neither do we see a Marxist exploitation of the poor. Both theories cause humans to be dominated by a few and for those being dominated this would not be Paradise. Humans are meant to display the innocence of human nature as the image of a holy and just God, each person sharing their gifts and talents without prejudice for the good of all and the glory of God. This is what the practical expression of the paradise of God looks like.

Paradise is where human relations are perfect and complimentary, each one acknowledging that we all are made as the imagers of God. The Gospel emphatically conveys the concept of racial equality from a God who loves and made us all. Just as a sidebar, when people say they do not know why God loves them, the reason is because He made us. Again, leaving no room for one to feel or act superior or inferior to anyone else.

God is good, just, and holy, and wants humans to demonstrate those same attributes. God as the Creator of humanity expected humans to get along and love each other. This requires that all humans love God first—and if we do, we will love each other as we love ourselves. The nature of God in humans requires that we watch out for each other and that all resources are stewarded in a way that the needs of all are met. Those who have prospered through talent, opportunity, or even preferential treatment should always have a strategy of being generous with a portion of their wealth, to supplement the legitimately poor and less fortunate. This is not socialism, but godly, voluntary and right living.

CHAPTER TWO

DIVINE DRAMA ACT 2:
DOCTRINE OF THE FALL

What Went Wrong?

The next major episode in the metanarrative is the fall of humankind and creation. The divine record of this event is found in Genesis 3. This is a critical piece of the Gospel because as the creation story answers the question, Why are we here? The fall event answers the question, What went wrong? Adam as the first human being created by God is dubbed the federal representative of humanity. This means Adam represented the whole human race as he lived out his probationary period in the Garden of Eden. The consequences of Adam's right or wrong decisions would therefore fall upon everyone. He was made as the imager of God and was to have dominion over all the earth under the sovereignty of God, his Creator. He was told to be fruitful and multiply, which led to the birth of humanity.

Adam received one prohibition from the Lord found in Genesis 2:17, which reads *"but of the tree of the knowledge of good and evil you shall not eat, for in the day that you eat of it you shall surely die."* The tree of the knowledge of good and evil was off limits for Adam's scope of freedom. God warned him unequivocally that if he ate he would die. This is where Satan first enters the scene, as the serpent, to seduce and deceive Adam and Eve. The Bible teaches that Satan was created as a free moral agent, along with all the other angels. He lost his position in Heaven because of his pride and rebellion against God. His only goal against God is to destroy the humans made as the image of God on earth. His strategy is to separate humans from covenant relationship with their Creator. Satan is a creature with limitations and Jesus records in the New Testament that *"The thief comes only to steal and kill and destroy ...*" John 10:10. So the answer to the question of what went wrong is that evil entered the world through the sin of Adam under the influence of Satan.

Listening to the serpent, Adam and his wife Eve ate of the tree of the knowledge of good and evil in spite of God's instructions; this act of disobedience possessed larger consequences than Adam could have ever imagined. Through Adam's act of disobedience, the whole human race fell into sin (Romans 5:12). Sin, *hamartia* in Greek, means missing or falling short of the mark. Adam did not immediately die, but physical death was inevitable. The biblical genealogy shows the progression of death in the human experience as our age span became truncated. Spiritual death was the immediate result of sin, and this had to do with fellowship with the Creator. This is why the sin in the garden is called the fall.

When one considers issues like earthquakes, floods, hurricanes, droughts, volcanic eruptions and tornadoes, etc. the question arises again, What went wrong? The

Gospel story answers this question with the pronouncement of God's judgment upon Adam. Genesis 3:17b reads
"... Cursed is the ground because of you..." The paradise
of Eden was lost through sin and even nature itself was
affected. The world now experiences what is called natural
evil as well as moral evil.

Adam and Eve decided to become their own gods,
therefore making their own decisions, no longer choosing
to obey God's word, but choosing to make their own
choices. As a result of the fall, the biblical worldview of
humanity is that all humans are born crooked, fallen, evil,
but through common grace can behave with civility. The
imagers of God have been distorted but not totally
destroyed. Antithetical to this is the modern worldview
that humans are basically good, and progress is inevitable.
However, as we survey the breadth of human relationships, especially among civilizations throughout history,
the modern worldview fails, as it is clear that something
has gone horribly wrong. Why do we treat each other the
way we do? Why do we view and judge each other the way
we do? What is the reason one ethnicity would decide to

practice genocide against another? Why does a caste system or classism among an ethnic group develop? Is one group of people inherently superior to another group? What is the source of the hostility, racism, discrimination, and prejudice? Understanding the fall answers these questions.

The story of Adam and Eve is not fiction or mythological. Anyone viewing the evil, suffering, injustice and death on this planet cannot come up with a better, more rational explanation than the biblical account. Sin has affected every aspect of human existence and function. Since the imaging of God has been marred and is now distorted, this means that our social skills, intellectual acuity, emotional health and physical health are damaged. We have lost our original function as the imagers of God. Human nature was made good (Genesis 1:31) but, Adam's disobedience plunged all humanity into sin. Humanity is now missing the mark for what God originally intended. We now have a propensity for evil and a serpent, the devil influencing us towards evil. We cannot correct ourselves or dig our way out of this pit. This is because not only did Adam sin, he also took on a new identity: a sinful nature. Now all of us are born into the world with a sinful nature and are incapable of rescuing ourselves from a gulag of self-destructive behavior. This is called original sin. Part of that self-destructive behavior is exhibited in the way we mistreat each other.

The Birth of Ethnocentrism

The ultimate expression of God's nature reflected in humanity is racial harmony, based on equality of worth and purpose. It is obvious that due to God's nature, He likes variety. He demonstrates this through creation's diversification in the same species or family of plants, animals and humans. The unity/diversity paradigm finds its roots in the very nature of God. God the Father, God the Son and God the Holy Spirit are one but three which is called hypostatic union.

In John 17, Jesus prayed that we would be one as He and the Father are one. This means that although the Father and the Son are distinct in personality, they are inseparable in essence and love. This is the example that

God has provided for us as humans. We are inseparable as a human race, yet distinct in ethnicity. In other words, God made us to love who He made us to be, but to also love others who have distinct differences from us. This is a divine concept that all Christians should embrace and cherish. The Bible says in Romans 15:7, *"Therefore welcome one another as Christ has welcomed you, for the glory of God."* He has taken us all in without reservation or prejudice.

One of the consequences of the fall is called ethnocentrism. This means that one ethnicity believes that they are superior to another ethnicity. The fall separated humans from God. Intimate communion with God was broken and the God-like image in humans was distorted. The fall left humans in a state of self-alienation. We cannot understand ourselves let alone someone else. This also opens the door for distorted self-love or narcissism. It is no wonder humans cannot get along. God's creation, that He once called very good, had now become evil. Not only is the fall the reason for evil, suffering, injustice and death, it is the reason for feelings and actions of hatred by humans toward each other even for no apparent reason. The practice of making assumptions and sweeping generalizations, which are informal fallacies in logic, are all part of the fall. This means ethnocentrism is not only sinful but also irrational.

Much effort is given to developing and maintaining an upper-class society or caste system. Even in the Black community, we have what is called the "Jack and Jill society", light-skinned Blacks choosing not to fellowship with darker Blacks, lest it hurt their social status among Whites. Their goal is to blend in to the society as much as possible. All of this is the result of sin, dehumanization and miseducation. The phrase, "person of color" is now popular when referring to non-Whites. Genetics prove that we are all from one color, that being brown. We are simply different shades of brown according to the activity of the pigment melanin in one's skin. (Ham and Ware 2010, 94).

The practice of ethnocentrism that produces racism, discrimination and prejudice are all part of the fall of man and clearly demonstrate its reality. This is not the work of God, but the work of fallen humanity under the influence of Satan. The worst expression of the depravity is that which has been expressed in the Church. In an interview with Bill Moyers on November 23, 2007, James Cone states, "racism is the original sin of the White church of America." (http://www.pbs.org/moyers/journal/1123200 7/transcript1.html) It is also true that in reaction to slavery and ongoing practices of prejudice by Whites, many in the Black church are prejudiced toward the White church. This is one of the greatest hindrances to the Church and its witness about the love of Christ for the world.

Cain and Abel: The Birth of Hatred

The Old Testament is replete with examples of one person thinking they are better than another or hating another person and therefore attempting to kill or enslave them. The first recorded act of murder is found in Genesis 4:8, "*Cain spoke to Abel his brother and when they were in the field, Cain rose up against his brother Abel and killed him.*"

In this account of two brothers, Cain fails to offer to God proper worship and was angered that God accepted Abel's offering and not his. Cain's anger and jealousy led him to kill his brother. Cain broke fellowship with God and once that fellowship was broken, the next step is breaking fellowship with other humans.

Self-hatred is part of the fall and if people cannot love themselves we cannot expect them to love others, even of the same ethnicity. The rest of Scripture reads like a Greek tragedy with the subsequent actions of humans killing each other for ungodly reasons. Just prior to the flood we find in Genesis 6:5 that *"The LORD saw that the wickedness of man was great in the Earth, and that every intention of the thoughts of his heart was only evil continually."* God describes the earth as full of violence by humans and God called it wickedness. This is the basis of unjust wars in the world; that men are wicked by nature and act upon the impulses of evil to their own destruction and the destruction of others. Just look at our present world, continents, states, cities, neighborhoods and families. There is violence everywhere. The enemy comes to kill, steal, and destroy (John 10:10).

The fact that one human would kill another is tragic enough, but one brother killing his own brother is unimaginable in a utopia. What is murder, other than the total disregard for the sacredness of life? It is an affront to God because He is the author of life. As created beings, we step into God's role when we assume the responsibility of making the ultimate decision for who lives and dies. Capital punishment is taught in the Word, but it only works properly when carried out under God's supervision. Corrupt men and systems have killed innocent people intentionally. The underlying factor in the story of Cain and Abel is the idea of jealousy and hatred. How deep these emotions must cut into the heart of God, that we would despise someone that He loves. How could we participate in an attitude that is irrational and counter-productive, except for the fact that we are fallen?

The Fall of Nature and
the Ethnic Domination of Resources

One has only to watch the news to hear of the many natural disasters around the world. These disruptions of nature are called natural evil. Some say if God is loving and all-powerful, He would not allow this natural evil to happen to innocent children. The biblical response is that God is loving and all-powerful, but sin entered the world through humans and Satan because both were created as free moral agents. Wrong choices created the fall and nature itself was affected in that the perfect harmony of creation was disturbed. This shows that man does have dominion over the earth and universe to some extent and that we can influence nature for good or bad. As Adam had the ground cursed for his sin and consequently nature began working against him, we live in a world where the laws of nature sometime work against us and cause terrible results for human life. It is also clear in Scripture that God can use nature to help us against our enemies or to discipline us because of our willful disobedience. God promised Israel that if they obeyed Him, He would give them the rain in season so the crops would grow. Conversely, He promised drought if they disobeyed (Deuteronomy 28:24).

When we look at the Garden of Eden text, God gave humans dominion over nature itself; however, since the fall, it is understood that the earth only possesses a limited set of resources. This becomes the challenge, to access and distribute these resources for the benefit of all humans. The fall brought a complication to the stewardship of resources. Men began to hoard and deny each other access to the resources based on prejudice, greed and a desire to control others. In a world where there is plenty for everyone, sin has brought moral evil into play, which can be deadly to those being denied.

One perfect example of the perversion of the dominion mandate is the continent of Africa. Many European nations infiltrated Africa to take advantage of her resources. Europe had depleted her own natural resources and was on the verge of collapse when they took over large portions of Africa and exploited the resources to their own advantage. They never had any intention of improving the lot of the Africans but did bring them the Bible. An African proverb says, "When the White man came we had the land and they had the Bible. Now we have the Bible and they have our land." Although the author of this statement cannot be identified, history validates its truth. Just think of what the Berlin Conference of 1884 did to Africa by dividing up the land across tribal boundaries. They instigated tribal warfare to their own advantage and the African tribes' destruction. All this they did for the resources of the land with total disrespect for the indigenous people.

The Gospel of Common Ancestry

It would be beneficial to look at the origin of the multiple ethnicities that have evolved upon the earth. How is it that from two people, Adam and Eve, we have so many people groups in the world? The Bible makes it very clear about the common origin of all nations. *"And He made from one man every nation of mankind to live on all the face of the Earth, having determined allotted periods and the boundaries of their dwelling place"* (Acts 17:26).

It should be reiterated that the Bible teaches that all humans have the same parents, Adam and Eve. But everyone was destroyed in the flood except Noah and his family, which included his wife, three sons, and their wives. Genesis 10 is entitled by some as the Table of Nations and verse 32 states, *"These are the clans of the sons of Noah, according to their genealogies, in their nations, and from these the nations spread abroad on the earth after the flood."* In this table, the genealogy of Noah's sons is presented in three divisions of the human race. It appears that the Jewish race comes from Shem; the Caucasian race comes from Japheth and the Black race comes from Ham.

So, it is after the flood that we see something genetic began to happen to the descendants of Noah's three sons; for all the nations of the earth evolved from them. We see that God had every intention of populating the earth with diversity among humans. The genealogies of Shem, Ham, and Japheth are biblical proof that we are all God's children, and that our diversity is a God-idea to be celebrated. It is also proof that God is the author of microevolution, meaning change within a species. The Bible attests to the truth that we are one human race with multiple ethnicities. This presents the most commonsense approach to our existence.

The secular scientists believe in evolution by time and chance for their macroevolution viewpoint on the origin of life. This belief has played a huge role in the sin of ethnocentrism since its origin. Basically, according to Charles Darwin and the chain of being theory, we are not of equal worth. The survival of the fittest has been a philosophy that justified ethnic cleansing around the globe. It is a pernicious doctrine from the pit of hell that degrades humanity to being equal with animals. This can only be the work of the devil, who would destroy all of us any way he can.

Current interpretations of Darwin's *Descent of Man* by Ham and Ware have answered the question, "Who is human and what is not?" (Ham and Ware 2007, 22–23). Some interpretations say that the breed of monkey you came from determines your intelligence among the ethnicities. This social Darwinism is partially responsible for the present attitude from Europe to the United States, that Blacks are the White man's burden due to being evolved from the least intelligent ape. This theory was purported by the book *The Bell Curve: Intelligence and Class Structure in American Life* (Richard J. Herrnstein and Charles Murray, 1994). It proposes that Blacks have less intelligence than Whites or other ethnicities.

The Curse of Ham

The fall caused the sin of ethnocentrism, which some have justified by Scripture from the account of Ham in Genesis 9. Here we find that Ham's son Canaan is cursed by Noah, because Ham looked upon his father's nakedness and reported it to his brothers, Shem and Japheth. Noah tells Ham that Canaan will be a slave to his brothers. The book of Joshua gives witness to the fulfillment of Noah's pronouncement when Israel defeats the Canaanites and makes them their slaves.

This text has been misinterpreted to mean all descendants of Ham, which is the entire Black race, are to be slaves for the rest of mankind. This is said to be God's judgment for all generations. However, they miss the fact that Ham had several sons, of which only one was cursed. So, if the curse was limited to Canaan and his descendants, which represents only part of the Black race, then why do some generalize this curse to include all of Ham's other sons and the entire Black race? The idea that all Ham's descendants were cursed became part of the justification for enslaving the African.

This is what the discipline of hermeneutics calls *eisegesis*, where one reads into the text what one wants to see according to their own biases or agendas. Nothing is as blinding as the sin of racism. The Bible can be twisted by anyone to justify a certain position, and such is the case with the curse of Ham (Genesis 9). It is surprising that both Jewish and Christian scholars have twisted this text to the detriment of not only Blacks, but themselves as well. This false sense of superiority, called white supremacy, has blinded many of European descent to think more highly of themselves than they should. This is the basis of colonialism and imperialism. Considering the level of exegetical skills possessed by biblical scholars, it is amazing that such weak interpretation has been demonstrated for this text. This proves that no one is totally free from cultural bias, not even the educated. Men such as Charles Darwin, George Hegel, Immanuel Kant, and Carl Linnaeus promoted the idea of white supremacy in their day and this wicked imagination is still alive today.

Nimrod the Warrior

In Genesis 10, Nimrod is called a mighty hunter before the Lord. The interesting point in this is that Nimrod is a descendent of Ham, and Scripture speaks favorably of him as the world's first builder of cities and empires. This historical truth goes a long way in demonstrating the equality of the ethnicities before God. It speaks to the tremendous intelligence and skill level that a Black person can possess, along with all other people. Such innovation and skill refutes any theory concerning the Black man's inability to think at high levels. It also negates the lie that has been perpetrated that Europeans and Asians are of a higher intellect. Aristotle's dictum saying that "some men are born to be the tools of slavery" is a monstrous, classist statement by the great philosopher. This shows that man, with all his intellectual ability, is still flawed, distorted, and in need of God to deliver him.

Tower of Babel: Human Diaspora

The story of the tower of Babel is found in Genesis 11:1, which reads: *"Now the whole earth had one language and the same words."* The text reveals that up until this point in human history, everyone spoke the same language. Humanity once again showed its fallen nature by trying to build a tower to Heaven perhaps in an effort to avoid another flood, as in Genesis 7. The purpose for the tower was to make a name for themselves and as an avenue for the gods to come down so they could worship them. God deemed it evil and diversified their languages.

The propensity of humankind's fallen nature is to pervert the gifts of God in our lives. Instead of giving glory to God, they sought to exalt humanity. This is the Enlightenment practice of exalting humanity above Deity. God judged the people due to their sin of pride and confusion was the result.

Good communication is the key to any relationship, and at the tower of Babel many relationships were lost. This loss initiated segregation and thus dispersion throughout the earth due to a language barrier. Look at all the languages spoken in the world today and the huge effort required by linguists to establish good communication. Consider the effort put into communication by way of translations because of the language barrier throughout human history. We have enough trouble communicating clearly within the same language, let alone in different languages. The fall of humanity progressively destroys relationships. Sin has made everything in life more difficult.

The Racial Nature of Israel

In Genesis 12, God called a man named Abram to leave his surroundings and family to fulfill the calling of God on his life. This began the birthing of a nation called Israel through the line of Shem. Abram became the first patriarch. God even specifies the geographical location of the land His people of Israel would inherit. Abram's wife was named Sarai. God promised that from their marriage a son would be born to bring about the promise of God. As his story progresses, Abram goes through many trials as God was preparing him to be the father of many nations— but still no son.

In Genesis 16 Abram and Sarai, after many years of waiting, still do not have a child. This barrenness causes great consternation in Abram's life and in desperation, he diverts from the promise of God. Sarai suggests that he has a child with her servant Hagar. This is an alternative route to produce the son of promise. The obvious fact of this story is that Hagar is an Egyptian who produces a child from Abram. This interrelationship brings together two different ethnicities, descended from Shem and Ham. Note that God denies this arrangement for the son of promise— but does promise Hagar that her son Ishmael will be blessed.

Joseph in Egypt with an Egyptian Wife

From the patriarchs Abraham, Isaac, and Jacob came a son named Joseph, who was sold into slavery by his brothers and ended up in an Egyptian jail. God delivered him from the jail by giving him the interpretation of Pharaoh's dream in Genesis 41. Pharaoh then exalted Joseph to second in command in Egypt and gave Joseph his daughter Asenath in marriage. This means that a descendant of Shem married a descendant of Ham.

This arrangement was political in nature, but demonstrates that had God been against interracial marriages, this would have been a good time to stop it. God orchestrated this event in Joseph's life, knowing he would end up in an interracial marriage. God not only blesses Joseph but out of this interracial marriage gives him two sons from whom two tribes of Israel come: Ephraim and Manasseh. And under the direction of God, Jacob, the patriarch speaks a blessing over these two sons of Joseph (Genesis 48:8-20) and they both received inheritance in the land of promise.

At the very heart of the nation of Israel, we find them not to be a pure ethnicity. Therefore, it can be deduced that God is not against interracial marriages. And since God blessed these two sons of Joseph, we can reason that He does not condemn but has condoned such a marital practice. He only forbids *inter-religious* marriages. God was concerned that it would cause Israel to serve foreign gods.

Exodus: The Mixed Multitude

In the book of Exodus, we have the story of Moses bringing deliverance to the children of Israel from under the hand of Pharaoh. It is stated in the text that they came out a mixed multitude on their way to the Promised Land (Exodus 12:38). This implies that Egyptians mingled with Hebrews and this led to friendships and potential marriages. If God was against the races mixing, He could have easily prevented the mixed multitude from leaving Egypt. This would have been a strategic moment to deal with it by purging Israel.

The truth is that God only speaks against marriages when there are different gods involved. Scripture says, *"Do not be unequally yoked with unbelievers [...]"* (2 Corinthians 6:14). The God of Israel required that His people, the nation of Israel, not mingle with other races due to the false gods that they worshiped (Deuteronomy 13:6-18). God was concerned that Israel would stray from Him, and several times they did. The one circumstance that God would honor the mixing of races was when the pagans converted to the Hebrew God.

Also noteworthy, God divided the very nation of Israel into tribes. He wanted all twelve tribes to live in the Promise Land. The segregation was not because one tribe was better than another; God divided them according to their inheritance in the land (Joshua 14-19). Specific boundaries were given for each tribe according to the land they were to possess. It was not a matter of race, since all twelve tribes were Hebrews.

Moses's Cushite Wife

In the book of Numbers 12, Moses has married an Ethiopian woman. His siblings, Aaron and Miriam, rebelled against his leadership as a result. They declared that Moses was not the only one who hears from God, and that they were disgusted by his interracial marriage. When the Lord spoke to the situation, He smote Miriam with leprosy and put her out of the camp for seven days. However, the Lord is silent about the issue of Moses's interracial marriage. Moses was married to a descendant of Ham, and he is a descendant of Shem. Throughout the Scriptures, God never gives the impression that He disapproved of Moses's marriage.

It is interesting that Miriam is struck with leprosy like snow (Numbers 12:10). The reality of Scripture reveals that when a person was cursed of God, the skin turns white. It is a fact that whiteness, at least for Miriam, is the result of God's displeasure. Nowhere in the Bible does it say, when God was displeased with Ham, He turned him black. It seems if that were Ham's curse, the Bible would say (like the instances of Miriam and others) that God turned them white. One conclusion of comparison is that blackness is not the result of the curse of Ham however, the reverse may be a truer conclusion.

Another interesting point to consider is the socio-economic plight of Israel, Egypt, and Ethiopia. The Egyptians and Ethiopians were the higher class of society and the Israelites were slaves. We see the contrast of the suburbs and the ghetto. When the events of Numbers 12 take place, the Cushites were the upper class, so Moses had married "up" in society, not down. This dispels the unexpressed interpretation by Whites that Blacks are always the lower class. In fact, the Egyptians were civilized at a time when the Greeks and British were still barbarians.

David and Bathsheba

David was considered one of the greatest leaders Israel ever had; his genealogy is mixed. His great great-grandmother was Rahab, a Canaanite. The Canaanites were from the descendants of Ham. Not only did David have a Hamitic bloodline, he also married a Philistine named Bathsheba, who was a direct descendant of Ham (2 Samuel 11:26–27; Genesis 10:14). To be technical, the name Bathsheba means daughter of Sheba. She was originally married to Uriah the Hittite, of the Canaanites (2 Samuel 11:3).

One of the worst stories of the fallen state of humans amongst God's people was when David committed adultery with Bathsheba and had Uriah killed to cover it up. Notice the severity of judgment that God brings against David. His family suffered many tragedies from that day forward as punishment for his murder and adultery. Yet, not once does the text mention that God was angry because Bathsheba was a descendant of Ham. The issue of color in the Church today was not an issue in the ancient world.

David and Solomon

Notice that the son of the mixed marriage between David and Bathsheba was Solomon. He was the next king of Israel and human co-author of the book of Song of Solomon. In Song of Solomon 1:5, the maiden states, "*I am black but comely.*" Cain Hope Felder, professor of New Testament Languages and Literature at Howard University Divinity School, states in *The Original African Heritage Bible*:

> The KJV among others here reflects an adversative "but comely" despite the fact that the original Greek

text uses a standard conjunction "and." This is one of the few places in the Bible where color is an issue instead of the culture. When she makes this statement it is a proactive response based on standards reflecting noble human and personhood values. This could be called the biblical "I'm black and I'm proud" statement (Felder 1993, 991).

While the correct interpretation of this Bible verse seems to affirm the positive outlook of the maiden about the color of her skin, translators who were European scholars skewed the verse in a negative light, using the conjunction "but" instead of "and", giving the reader the impression that the maiden felt being black was undesirable. This is an instance where scholars allowed their prejudice to influence their interpretation. It is hard for even Christians to be totally objective when it comes to interpreting the Scriptures.

Race in the New Testament:
The Mixed Genealogy of Jesus

There seems to be no hint of prejudice in the Old Testament based on skin color. Typically, slavery was the result of war or debt. The winners of a war simply made slaves out of the losers. If you had debt you could not pay, you could become an indentured servant to pay what you owed by working. The discrimination in that day was based on ethnicity, not color. Although the racism of our present day was not systematic back then, seeds of it can be traced back to the fifth and sixth century B.C. where people began to be valued by environmental factors such as climate and geography (Isaac 2004, 55-56).

As the New Testament was unfolding, the historian William Barclay states, "The Jews had an immense contempt for the Gentile" (Barclay 1976, 107). Like in the Old Testament, the sin of the era was the sin of contempt between ethnicities. The Romans, Greeks, Samaritans, and the Jews all hated each other, and the Jews were the most despised. Among the Jews, those of the north were not favorable toward those in the south and vice versa. When traveling to Jerusalem, Jews would cross over the Jordan to avoid the Samaritans. This made the trip longer, but that is the lengths to which prejudice will cause one to go. Racial prejudice is not an invention of the modern world, it is a social construct. Jesus was born into a fallen world full of the darkness of racism to which He brought the light.

The Jews put a high premium on a person's lineage; priests had to have proof of their heritage to be in the priesthood. Despite this, we instantly find a mixture in the genealogy of Jesus presented in the book of Matthew. The overarching providence of God leads to the meeting between Ruth, the Moabite, and Boaz. Tragedy struck leaving both Naomi and her daughter-in-law Ruth widowed and heading back to Israel to be closer to family. Due to their humble living situation, Ruth goes out to glean food in the fields. Boaz, the landowner and relative of Naomi, notices Ruth and looks upon her with favor. After going through proper protocol of a kinsman redeemer, Boaz takes Ruth as his wife.

Rahab, the previously mentioned Canaanite was a harlot from of the city of Jericho. She is also included in the lineage of Jesus. From Joshua 6, we find that the original spies of Israel went into Jericho. It was Rahab who hid them and helped them escape from the city. In turn, the spies promised Rahab she would be spared when the city was destroyed. This again is the providence of the Almighty, protecting His people and setting up the future relatives for the lineage of Jesus. Ethnically speaking then Jesus was a person of mixture because at least two of the five women, Rahab and Bathsheba, mentioned in Matthew's genealogy are of Hamitic origin and Ruth was a Moabite.

In the redemptive plan of God in the earth, the New Testament finds the expectation of Israel awaiting the coming of the Messiah. But the kind of world He is birthed into is quite racially charged. Each ethnic group considered the other *persona non grata*, an unacceptable or unwelcome person. Let's remember though, at that time, racial prejudice was not about the color of your skin, but ethnic prejudice is sin, nevertheless.

Amid this ethnocentrism, the Savior who comes from a mixed bloodline is born. Ruth, Rahab and Bathsheba in the lineage of Jesus proved that it is God's intent to mix races for His eternal purposes. The implication could be that in the purposes of God, it is a matter of the heart rather than a matter of ethnicity or the color of the skin. Again, this is a reflection of God's nature. He is not a racist; He is making a statement of His indiscriminate love for all His creation. If this is the nature of God, and it is, then His Church ought to reflect that nature through incarnational ministry. American churches have not done this with any major effort but remain complicit. The power of the Holy Spirit can deliver us all from an evil heart. We need to have sensitive, informed, and civil conversations. We need courage to bring down the wall of separation that exists in the Church between all ethnic groups, especially regarding the binary conflict between the Black and White churches. Jesus has judicially torn down the wall; we are empowered to experientially remove the wall by the preaching of the Gospel.

The Wise Men

In Matthew 2:1, it reads," *Now after Jesus was born in Bethlehem of Judea in the days of Herod the king, magi from the east arrived in Jerusalem.*" The wise men are recorded as coming from the East. At that time in history they would have all been of a darker complexion. Europeans possibly started to change all icons and religious paintings to white around the fourth century A.D. (Anyike 1995, 160) although one wise man has traditionally remained depicted as a Black man in present day Christmas decorations.

Simon of Cyrene

In Matthew 27:32, Jesus has been forced into carrying His cross beam on the Via Dolorosa. Along the way He understandably collapsed, and the soldiers sequestered a man called Simon of Cyrene to help Him. In the providence of God, He allows a Black man the privilege of assisting in the greatest act of God for humankind. This African was from Cyrene, a city in the providence of Cyrenaica, which is in present day Libya of North Africa. Cain Hope Felder comments in the *Original*

Heritage Bible, "Since Jesus Himself along with His family members and disciples were all of mixed racial stock as Afro-Asiatics, one need not become overly preoccupied with the extent to which Simon was a black man" (1993, 1431).

Pentecost: A Multi-Ethnic Experience

The Book of Acts proves to be a narrative text that is replete with examples of racial unity and dissention. On what some call the birthday of the early church in Jerusalem, a spiritual phenomenon took place. God poured out the Holy Spirit upon the people who had come to celebrate the feast of Pentecost. Acts 2:5 reads, *"Now there were dwelling in Jerusalem Jews, devout men from every nation under Heaven."* The demographics of the crowd on that feast day was very diverse. There were people from Turkey, the Mediterranean area, and several nations of North Africa (Egypt, Libya, and Cyrenaica). The North African nations mentioned are where the Hamitic people came from and the point to be made is simply this, Africans were present on the day of Pentecost.

Scripture says that the Lord poured out His Spirit upon people of all flesh. When the Holy Spirit came upon the disciples on the day of Pentecost, they were supernaturally empowered by God to speak in languages they did not learn, and the people that were present heard the words of the apostles as they spoke in other tongues about the mighty deeds of God, *opus Dei*. This was God showing everyone involved that He is for all people. Sin caused the languages to be divided in Genesis 11 at the tower of Babel, but the Holy Spirit can transcend all languages to cause all to understand.

God is intentional about all His creation being in right relationship with Him by hearing the Gospel. Peter says later in Acts 10:34–35, *"that God shows no partiality, 35 but in every nation anyone who fears him and does what is right is acceptable to him."* This text proves that Africans were a part of the original audience on the day of Pentecost, not some minority group that Europeans in later history brought the Gospel to for the first time.

The Ethiopian Eunuch

The Ethiopian eunuch is obviously African. He was a high official in charge of the treasury. This made him a man of great importance in his country. The story is recorded in Acts 8:26-39; note the spiritual significance. An angel talks to Philip and gives him directions that lead to the Ethiopian. The Ethiopian had just left Jerusalem, where he had been attending the feast of Pentecost. God obviously saw the sincerity of his heart and ordained for him to receive salvation. In this chapter, Luke annunciates the fact that the Holy Spirit led Philip to bring salvation to an African. This is scriptural proof once again that God is no respecter of persons, and certainly does not put Blacks in a separate and lower category than Whites. This also dispels the myth that Europeans introduced the Gospel to the Africans because this eunuch returned to Ethiopia and would have shared the Gospel that Philip shared with him. Thomas Oden in his book, *How Africa Shaped the Christian Mind: Rediscovering the African Seedbed of Western Christianity*, records Africa's influence in shaping the early church. In fact, leading to the Reformation it was Augustine from Tunisia's theology that shaped John Calvin and Martin Luther's theology. Most of the early African church leaders were called Latin fathers by the European church. This was because they wrote in Latin and it hid their ethnicity.

Peter at Cornelius's House

In Acts 10, the apostle Peter has a unique Holy Spirit experience. While in a trance, he has a vision having to do with the Jewish dietary laws. It was through their dietary laws that God taught Israel the difference between clean and unclean, holy and unholy. In the vision, three times Peter sees all kinds of animals, reptiles and birds and heard a voice saying to kill and eat. Peter responded by saying that he had never eaten anything common or unclean. The voice said to Peter, "What God has made clean, do not call common." Right after his vision, Peter received a request to go to the Gentile Cornelius' house. Israel under Roman rule, despised the Gentile world. They longed for the day that the Messiah would come and avenge them by defeating all their enemies. It was against this backdrop that God challenged Peter's disposition toward Gentiles, revealing to him that all humankind was the object of His redeeming love. Through His death and resurrection, God was reclaiming all His creation, of which Jews were not the only part.

When Peter comes to Cornelius's house he reveals God's dealings with him about his prejudice. Before Peter can finish his speech, the Holy Spirit is poured out on the Gentiles. It is then that Peter understands the love of God for all people. The outpouring of the Holy Spirit on the Gentiles was the same visible manifestation that Peter had experienced on the day of Pentecost and an absolute convincing evidence of equality among all people in the sight of God.

Peter had seen the truth of God, but the rest of the Jewish leaders and members were not there yet. In Acts 11, they reprimand Peter for eating with the Gentiles, and the debate is taken to Jerusalem for the council to decide where the Gentiles should be placed in the Church (Acts 15). The Holy Spirit educated the Jews that they were not the only ones accepted by God. The outcome of the Jerusalem meeting was that there should not be a caste system in the Church; the Gentiles were of equal status with the Jews in God's economy. Again, this witnesses to the nature and character of God, that He loves all. The Holy Spirit in the Book of Acts is always moving His Church toward evangelism and producing ethnic harmony.

Racial Leadership at Antioch

In Acts 13, Luke records the gathering of the leaders to pray for God's will concerning outreach to the Gentiles. This was a historic gathering because they transitioned from an exclusively Jewish outreach to now include the whole Gentile world.

Notice the racial plurality of the elders at Antioch. Two of the elders are from Africa; Simon called Niger (which means black man) and Lucius of Cyrene, which is in northern Libya. In initiating the evangelization of the Gentiles, God deemed it necessary to represent His love and acceptance of diverse people who repent and come to unity. This is a paradigm for the concept of diversity of leadership to reach the masses. There is no mention of a dispute regarding the racial diversity by any of the leaders and the Holy Spirit does not dispute the mixture either. In fact, the Holy Spirit speaks in their midst and gives specific directions for the growth of the Church.

Racism in the History of Western Civilization

In considering the impact of racism on the Gospel, a clear path can be seen in the history of western civilization. The concept of dualism was presented in Augustine's book, *The City of God* published in 426 A.D. This is the idea that somethings are under God's rule and somethings are independent of God's rule, that there is the *sacred and the secular* instead of all things being in God's kingdom and under His rule. Corruption came into practice when those who capitalized on the secular part became deistic in their worldview. Deists believe in the existence of God as the Creator but think that He remains distant from His creation. They reason that He allows His creation to manage itself through natural laws and that God does not get involved supernaturally with humankind. This understanding eventually leads to a position of white supremacy expressed in colonialism. The White secularists dropped the sacred and kept the secular, taking advantage of dualism to promote their own humanistic agenda (Translation, 1950). This agenda includes evolution, imperialism, and racism. This progression is seen in the book *Free at Last? The Gospel in the African-American Experience* by Carl Ellis, Jr. (1996). The Church lost her salt and allowed the biblical worldview to die a slow death, even as she was extending herself by landing on the shores of America.

It is also notable that the Church was participating in trying to reconcile the truth of the Bible with the philosophy of their day. Dr. Mark Noll addresses this issue in his book, *The Scandal of the Evangelical Mind.* He says that beginning around the 18th century, "...most evangelicals who took an interest in science, philosophy, history, politics, and the arts adopted procedures of the Enlightenment by which to express their thought in these areas" (Noll 1994, 83). The Enlightenment was an intellectual movement during the late 17th and 18th centuries in Europe focused on reason and individualism rather than traditional beliefs. Protestant educators chose to adopt this form of enlightenment to promote their position because it was the best rationalization that reflected theological truth in secular terms. This position gave White Americans a way to feel superior which had a detrimental impact on the Gospel in America and allowed for racism. The sense of manifest destiny prevailed in their psyche; they thought God made them superior to Blacks and Native Americans. This was called protestant supremacy first, which then evolved into white supremacy in America. (*Christian Slavery,* Katharine Gerber). This air of superiority in the colonial churches directly contributed to the split between the White and Black church. The White church in general completely ignored the mandates in Scripture to "*welcome one another as Christ has welcomed you for the glory of God*" (Romans 15:7).

One leader of our nation at that time was Abraham Lincoln. As noble as he appears in history, he was still a man of his times. Lincoln is quoted saying:

> I will say then that I am not, nor ever have been, in favor of bringing about in any way the social and

political equality of the white and black races - that I am not nor ever have been in favor of making voters or jurors of Negroes, nor of qualifying them to hold office, nor to intermarry with white people; and I will say in addition to this that there is a physical difference between the white and black races which I believe will forever forbid the two races living together on terms of social and political equality. And inasmuch as they cannot so live, while they do remain together there must be the position of superior and inferior and I as much as any other man am in favor of having the superior position assigned to the white race. I say upon this occasion I do not perceive that because the white man is to have the superior position the Negro should be denied everything. (http://avalon.law.yale.edu/19th_century/lincoln2.asp)

This mindset has had a devastating effect on our whole society. Believing one's own ethnicity is superior always has negative implications and is the result of oppression, wars and in this case, slavery. The enslaved

Africans were suffering from an inferiority complex, and Whites were suffering from a superiority complex. Either way demonstrates an inaccurate, unbiblical worldview and therefore, a fallen human condition.

It appears that the devil has it out for Black people. To validate slavery, some American denominations interpreted Genesis 4:15 that the mark of Cain was that his skin turned dark. This is a perverted slant toward the demoralization of Blacks. There is nothing in Genesis 4 that implies that Cain was turned black after he killed Abel. Cain's mark was from the Lord to protect him. It is particularly surprising though to find the Jewish writings of the Talmud and Midrash speaking pejoratively about blackness. In *Tractate Sanhedrin*, Epstein and translators write that the Babylonian Talmud says, "Our Rabbis taught: Three copulated in the ark, and they were all punished—the dog, the raven, and Ham. [...] and Ham was smitten in his skin" (Epstein, 1969). The explanatory footnotes further read that from Ham "was descended Cush (the Negro) who is black-skinned." Even God's people can be blinded by the sin of ethnocentrism.

It appears that Europeans backed into disrespecting the African, partially due to their cultural definition of blackness. The Oxford dictionary of the sixteenth century defines black to mean dirty, foul, and wicked. On the whole subject of color, it has to be understood that God created colors. We see in creation all the colors of the rainbow and in nature, a diverse spectrum of colors. Some colors are the result of combining the major colors, which once again displays the splendor of God's intent. It should also be noted that depending on the context, black could be used to represent good or bad. Many positive things are represented by blackness. The robes of academia, robes for justices of the court, and uniforms of police officers all represent something of respect and honor. So, where is the rub? What is causing the disconnect concerning Black history?

The great cover-up is an interesting phenomenon in the human history of racism and prejudice. European scholars covered up the facts of history, that Black people have made major contributions to the development of human civilization. The question begs to be asked, why would people who consider themselves to be superior and enlightened cover up the truth? Part of the answer is simply pride. Because of the generational attitude and cultural conditioning, the ego becomes so inflated that it would be a herculean task to humble oneself without the grace of God. This arrogant attitude has a beginning place in human history.

Egypt and her substantial contributions in history is a quintessential component in understanding the attitude of Europeans. Ancient historians write that the Egyptians were black. Psalm 105:23 calls Egypt the land of Ham. Rather than admit that so much of civilization's accomplishments originated in Africa, the White scholars and anthropologists' strategy was to cover up the truth and discredit the African people and their accomplishments. It would have required great humility and intellectual integrity to admit that all they had come to believe about their superiority to the Africans was a lie. Chancellor Williams does an excellent job in his book *The Destruction of Black Civilization*, detailing the strategic moves the anthropologists have made to cover up the facts (Williams, 1987). One of the greatest deceptions was their changing of the Egyptians into Europeans. The scholars purported that the Egyptians were white, not black. Africans at that time did not have the power or influence to counter Europe's multi-level schemes of self-proclaimed superiority.

In the realm of education and the subject of philosophy in particular, the origins must be reexamined. The idea of Socrates, Plato, and Aristotle discovering philosophy is a huge stretch considering the lack of evidence; arguments against this notion are much more plausible. The lack of objectivity and scholarship in Eurocentric hermeneutics concerning African knowledge of philosophy is appalling. From an Afrocentric hermen-eutic, the discovery of this truth is a tremendous identity boost of self-worth. The impact of this truth on a people considered the White man's burden, who have been shamefully dehumanized, cannot be measured.

The positive outcome of this discovery about Greeks not being responsible for the origin of philosophy is a topic of great discussion in the halls of academia today. It is time for some true scholarship and integrity on this issue. Both White and Black scholars need to address it, separately and collectively. This will require rewriting the history books after intense research by a diverse-members committee.

Racism in Darwinian Evolution

As many have attested, the theory of evolution changed the world in many ways. It became a "come out of the closet card" for atheists all over the world. Evolution has become the justification for excluding theism from the universities and from the field of science in particular. There is no way to measure the damage this one idea has perpetrated in history. It inevitably became the ultimate justification for racism, as well. Because of evolution, non-Black people felt they had scientific proof for their ideas of blackness and subsequent superiority over it. Furthermore, evolution is the justification for abortion mills in the Black community of America. Margaret Sanger, a eugenicist, was instrumental in spreading the message of racism and establishing abortion clinics in Black neighborhoods. Even among these practices, the Bible was used to justify racism.

In Chapter 19 of his book *America's God: from Jonathan Edwards to Abraham Lincoln*, Mark Noll (2002) explains how it was from the regulative principle of reformed theology that the Bible was used to justify slavery. Although this principle is valid for interpretation of Scripture, it is not the only principle to be considered. It appears that in the pre-Civil War period the slavery discussion was quite heated, and some of the great theologians wrestled with the issue. It was determined by America's best scholars that the Bible, and the New Testament in particular, endorsed slavery. Charles Hodge, the great Princeton scholar, wrote in an essay entitled, "The Fugitive Slave Act," in 1860:

> The obedience which slaves owe their masters, children their parents, wives their husbands, people their rulers, is always made to rest on the divine will as its ultimate foundation. It is part of the service which we owe to God... In appealing therefore, to the Bible in support of the doctrine here advanced,

we are not, on the one hand, appealing to an arbitrary standard, a mere statute book [...] but we are appealing to the infinite intelligence of a personal God, whose will, because of His infinite excellence, is necessarily the ultimate ground and rule of all moral obligation.

The American church was influenced by the imperialistic attitude of the day. They debated the question: If the slaves were converted to Christianity and become baptized can we still keep them as slaves? Obviously, they did not consider 1 Timothy 1:10 where Paul called enslavers (those who take someone captive in order to sell him into slavery) lawless, disobedient, ungodly, sinners, unholy and profane.

For the enslaved Africans, this presented a dilemma. How does a God who loves everyone endorse slavery of the African? Let's take a closer look at the ugly institution called slavery from a hermeneutical position. For instance, there is a principle called the redemptive-movement hermeneutic (Webb 2005, 382). Webb contends that we must look at the *letter* of the text and the *spirit* of the text. What he means is that if we just look at the letter, we may still misinterpret because we don't consider the redemptive spirit of the text. Pertaining to slavery, one must consider the ancient cultural setting. How is the Old Testament text showing any redemptive spirit? Whatever the social issue that God addresses with Israel, it is an improved moral position than that of the rest of ancient civilization. Webb says about the improvement of the Old Testament slavery code, "Scripture moved the cultural 'scrimmage markers' only so far downfield" (Webb 2005, 388). He is saying although an improvement to the practice of slavery progressed in the Old Testament there was still further to go in the New Testament.

An example of this scrimmage marker being moved is found in Exodus 21:16. Ancient nations stole people to sell them. God denounces the practice of these nations by telling Israel, that whoever kidnaps a person and sells them shall surely be put to death. Another example is that God required Israel to release slaves with some compensation (Deuteronomy 15:12–18). The Europeans must have skipped over these regulations as they considered the economic gain slavery would provide. This is a form of racism called the exploitation of capitalism.

At first glance, the slave codes of the Old Testament can be misinterpreted to show God as quite cruel, even inhumane. For instance, in Exodus 20, a slave could be beaten as long as he didn't die. Another example is found in Exodus 12, where slaves were considered property. When you add Paul's household codes on slavery (Ephesians 6:5-8, Colossians 3:22, Titus 2:9), it is no wonder that in the Americas, Christians thought it biblical to enslave people. But this is where the scholars have fallen short. They did not consider what William Webb explains as redemptive movement. He writes:

> Movement is a crucial component of meaning within the biblical text. In fact, an examination of biblical texts reveals various kinds of redemptive movement—*foreign movement* (in relation to the ancient culture) *domestic movement* (in relation to existing traditions or social norms within the immediate covenant community) and *canonical*

movement (across large epochs in salvation history, primarily from Old Testament to the New Testament) (Webb 2005, 387–388).

What was the antebellum canonical application of redemptive spirit movement? It is clear that had the White pro-slavery churches considered this hermeneutic —along with obeying the slave codes of the Old Testament about not beating, killing, and stealing people for trade— there would not have been such a tragic chapter in American history. This is part of the sad commentary of human history attesting to the fact that we are fallen in nature.

The Birth of the Black Church and Theology

It is a daunting horn of dilemma from the perspective of Black scholars and the Black church on the issue of slavery and God in His sovereignty allowing it. This has been their theological struggle from the inception of Black theology and the Black church. The technical term for this suffering is called theodicy, which means how God, being good and all-powerful, allows evil. Not only does God allow evil, it appears to happen to Black people disproportionately, more than to others. Some Blacks believe that our suffering is proof that God does not exist and if He does, He is a racist. William R. Jones states, "To speak of divine racism is to raise the question about God's equal love and concern for all men. It is to suggest that He is for some but not for others, or at least not for all equally" (Jones 1997, 6). Some argue that Blacks are from the 10 lost tribes of Israel and proof of Deuteronomy 28:64-68. A substantial number of Hebrews from the dispersion of the northern kingdom of Israel did migrate to Northwest Africa and the slave ships did take Africans from Northwest Africa to the Americas (Isaiah 11:11).

Since there is a separate institution called the Black church, what is its nature and mission? The Black community struggles with a double consciousness - a love and a hate relationship for America. There is also a divided mind in the Black church of America, that of piety and protest. The Black church has always borne witness to the Christian faith as expressed in the Apostles' Creed, so what is the difference from the White church? Let's begin with the nature of the Black church. From its inception, the Black church was birthed out of the struggle of slavery during the Second Great Awakening. Warnock states:

> The freedom for which the black church has fought has always been both internal and external, expressing itself politically and spiritually, embracing Black's bodies and souls. This is so because historically the faith of the black church has been shaped and characterized by two complementary yet competing sensibilities: revivalist piety and radical protest (Warnock 2014, 13).

There seems to be a rift between the Black church and its theologians. The tension comes from each side promoting a special emphasis. The Black church emphasis is revivalist piety, and the Black theologian's emphasis is social protest. When the Holy Spirit visited the enslaved Africans, this produced an overwhelming gratitude and sense of holiness in their understanding of God. Concomitant with this, the Holy Spirit produced a sense of justice in their lives, which produced radical protest. Moses brought social protest to Pharaoh on behalf of the children of Israel. Therefore, when seeking to understand the nature of the Black church, these earmarks, along with the Apostles' Creed, must be considered and embraced.

Along with this comes what Shelton and Emerson, in their book *Blacks and Whites in Christian America: How Racial Discrimination Shapes Religious Convictions* call the building blocks of the Black Protestant faith (Shelton and Emerson, 2012). There is first the *experiential* building block, which is to say the Black church is less doctrinal and more action oriented. Second is the *survival* building block, which is to say that through all the struggles, the Black church has carried the Black community. Third is the *mystery* building block, which deals with the fact that folklore and conjuring play a part in the liturgy of the Black church. Fourth is the building block of the miraculous as ordinary in Christian life. Finally, there is the building block of *social justice and equality* for all people (Shelton and Emerson 2012, 8). This last building block is where the greatest wall of separation between the Black and White churches exists. One of the main issues would be reparation. Israel came out with silver and gold, while the enslaved Africans came out without the forty acres and a mule General William T. Sherman promised on January 16, 1865.

In the Gospel message, the question of how we fix this should include recognition and understanding of the heresy of racism. How do we fix the injustices, inequalities, discrimination, and prejudice? It is the nature of the Black church to function in piety and protest. Concerning the birthing of Black theology, James Cone says:

> The origin of black theology has three major contexts: (1) the civil rights movement of the 1950s and '60s, largely associated with Martin Luther King, Jr.; (2) the publication of Joseph Washington's book, Black Religion (1964); and (3) the rise of the black power movement, strongly influenced by Malcolm X's philosophy of black nationalism (Cone 1984, 6).

Because of these three components, there must be loving, accurate, historical discussion about these three schools of thought for a relationship to be forged. The White church of America has to know and understand these things to make headway in the relationship. This should be called the second Reformation, for it was born out of the protest of evils against the White church of America. One of the main reasons for the protest was the hypocrisy of White slave owners who claimed to be Christian.

Frederick Douglass is one of the main heroes of the abolitionist movement. He had been a slave and then became free. He was the leading Black lecturer in the abolitionist movement. He states:

> It was in the month of August 1883, when I had become almost desperate under the treatment of Master Thomas, and entertained more strongly than ever the oft-repeated determination to run away, a circumstance occurred which seemed to promise brighter and better days for us all. At the Methodist camp-meeting, held in the Bayside (a famous place

for camp meetings) about eight miles from St. Michaels, Master Thomas came out with a profession of religion. [...] 'If he has got religion," thought I, "he will emancipate his slaves; or if he should not do so much as this, he will at any rate behave towards us more kindly, and feed us more generously than he has heretofore done.'[...] But in my expectations I was doubly disappointed: Master Thomas was Master Thomas still (Douglass 1983, 100).

From this excerpt Douglass shares with us that the conversion experience of Master Thomas only made him act worse toward Black folks. Due to this incident, Douglass makes the decision to run away because he saw no other positive recourse.

In his book *Black Theology in Dialogue*, Deotis Roberts shares, that even in the Pentecostal movement, with its primary emphasis on the Holy Spirit, there has been demonstrated a racist attitude toward the authenticity and birthing of the movement itself (Roberts 1987,

59). White scholars when writing about the movement's history in the United States relegate Black pioneers such as William J. Seymour to a sentence or footnote when their influence was worldwide.

A better definition of racism is provided by Joseph R. Barndt, who says, "racism is prejudice with power" (Barndt, 1991). From this definition, the White church should understand that although all can be prejudiced, only White America could be racist. From the inception of America, Whites have possessed power over Blacks through slavery, Jim Crowism, segregation, separate but equal, the GI Bill, and even the Fair Housing Authority, all of which demonstrate the systemic racism of White America. Racism comes with the power to withhold resources necessary for survival. Blacks have never been in a superior position in the history of America.

Shelton and Emerson, both sociologists, have done extensive research to find the distinctive hallmarks of the Black church in comparison to the White church. The research shows that Blacks do engage in all the Christian disciplines such as prayer and church attendance in expectation of miracles in greater measure than that of Whites. This is primarily due to suffering, discrimination, and racism from White America. This is not to suggest that Blacks inherently possess greater virtue than Whites, but that they have experienced greater persecution. It appears from Scripture that undeserved suffering can be redemptive, in a narrow sense. We see this in the Genesis 50 story of Joseph, who after being unjustly persecuted by his brothers and Potiphar's wife, became the second most powerful man in the world. In verses 19-20, Joseph says, *"Do not fear, for am I in the place of God? 20 As for you, you meant evil against me but God meant it for good, to bring it about that many people should be kept alive"* However, the whole subject of theodicy is a constant struggle for Black theologians. It is not that all other ethnicities have prospered or escaped oppression, but that Blacks have simply suffered more. The question is: why the disparity of suffering experienced by Blacks?

The Black church is struggling with her identity and function in the Black community and broader society.

From an apologetic position, the Black church must also come to grips with this struggle to combat the Islamic pull on the Black community, and especially the Black man. The particular draw of the Nation of Islam is the demonization of the White race and exaltation of the Black race. It is through leaders such as Malcolm X, who spoke truth to power and exposed the evil of racism, that the Black community was increasingly attracted to the Muslim movement. Malcolm X preached the beauty of the Black race and courageous opposition to the White race of America. This he did at a time when most Blacks were afraid of white power, speaking only privately against Whites. He spoke to a Black people loosed from physical chains, but still bound psychologically and economically. The Black church must explain to Black America, like Frederick Douglass did, that Black Christians are committed to the Christ of Scripture, not the Christ of White America.

Dr. Cain Hope Felder has done the Black church and Black theology a great service in his rendition of *The Original African Heritage Study Bible* (Felder, 1993). In this Bible, the African Christian story is told in its true historical context portraying historically accurate pictures from Bible times. The Black church, when it purchases church buildings due to white flight, should remove all pictures and icons painted with White angels and White Jesus. This is necessary for Blacks' healthy self-image and refuting the argument that Christianity is the White man's religion. In western civilization, Jesus on the cross is white. Why is there not a brown or Black Jesus on the cross? When people say that color doesn't matter, tell that to all the artists who have painted Jesus as white.

When it became public that Reverend Jeremiah Wright was president Obama's pastor, the nation exploded, not understanding Black theology. This was a national indicator that the White majority does not yet understand the Black minority. History is important to both Blacks and Whites. Concerning the white version of Black American history, Randall Robinson best explains it. He states:

> It is as if, since its very establishment, America had chosen to hold, as Napoleon would, that "history is

the myth that men choose to believe." The crypto-Machiavellians who serve as the perennial stewards of American public affairs understand that people on the whole are about as malleable as their history can be made to be. The landscape is rife with examples, from historically overarching lies and half-truths to popular culture deceits (Robinson 2000, 33).

Robinson describes the Black race as history's amnesiacs, because we live with the memories of others. Robinson also states, "No people can live successfully, fruitfully, triumphantly without strong memory of their past, without reading the future within context of some reassuring past, without implanting reminders of that past in the present" (Robinson 2000, 27). When God brought Israel out of Egypt to Mt. Sinai, the first thing he taught them through Moses was the knowledge of their history and God in it. Whites and Blacks know all about Western civilization and by the way, prejudice can be taught by what you don't say. Education in this country would serve our nation better if the good and bad of all races was taught. That way, no one group could possibly have an elevated opinion of themselves above the others. We have all done great things, but we all have a history of doing very bad things, too. We are all equal when it comes to the fall of humankind.

This dilemma has gone on for so long that many are tired of trying to fix it, though a few attempts have been made. The Promise Keepers organization is one example of a Christ-centered ministry that tried and failed to reconcile the Church. Why do such attempts fail? In the case of the Promise Keepers, it is likely because asking for forgiveness and giving forgiveness in a stadium setting falls short of real relationship building and problem-solving.

CHAPTER THREE

DIVINE DRAMA ACT 3:
DOCTRINE OF REDEMPTION

How Do We Fix It?

The third act of the Gospel is called redemption, which speaks to the philosophical question: How do we fix it? Ever since the fall the divine drama has repeatedly shown us how crooked and broken we are; and no matter how hard we try, we cannot fix it. We find in the redemption story the good news that He, speaking of Jesus, can fix it.

Before God puts Adam out of the garden, He gives him a promise that the future is not all lost. The Gospel of Christ first appears in Genesis 3:15, where God promises a redeemer: *"I will put enmity between you and the woman, and between your offspring and her offspring: he shall bruise your head, and you shall bruise his heel."* This is a reference to the coming Messiah who will defeat Satan. Adam and Eve leave the garden under punishment, yet with hope for the future.

As the Creator and Sustainer of the universe and humanity, Jesus came into this world to save what had been lost. Jesus is the God who showed up. The Incarnation, (explained in 1 Timothy 3:16 as Jesus who was fully God became fully Man), was the only way to rescue nature and humanity from the fall. Jesus created us, and it is Jesus who had to pay the price to purchase us back, for He is the spotless innocent Lamb of God. Everything was lost in the Garden of Eden. An angel kept guard at the entrance preventing Adam from returning to the garden, because it was a sacred space for the divine council room on earth. The second Adam (Jesus) has reopened the garden through His life, death, and resurrection. If we could do it ourselves, we would not need a savior.

The Scriptures teach that we are dead in sin; and a dead man cannot assist in his own resurrection. Jesus understands us and as the mediator, He shows us how we are to live on earth and what God is like. We must repent and surrender our will to the Lord, for He is the only one who can raise us from the dead, back to life. The word *repent* means to change your mind, and that is what we must do. All must be submitted to the Lordship of Jesus Christ. This is an act that can only be initiated by the Holy Spirit. It is called being born again or born from above. It is through this rebirth experience that we are restored back into a right relationship with God.

Redemption and Racism

The Jewish understanding of redemption is not only deliverance from sin, guilt, and shame, but also the deliverance from *the sin of human-imposed oppression* and everything that stood in the way of the community's productive life. The Black church born in America under slavery agrees with the Jewish understanding of redemption. The White church expresses and teaches the first half of the definition, leaving out deliverance from human oppression. So, what did the White preachers teach the slaves? Olin Moyd states:

> While this position is theologically sound, it is equally conspiratorial in that it is limited to salvation from the eternal consequences of sin, meaning those consequences beyond death. The theology in this sermon intentionally neglects to admit that redemption has its genesis in salvation from the state or circumstances, which destroy human values and existence in this world. (Moyd 1979, 39).

Since the Holy Spirit played such a major role in the conversion of the enslaved African, there is great need to continue to rely upon Him for all things spiritual and social. After all, it was through the second Great Awakening, Finney's revival, and the Azusa Street Revival that God liberated the enslaved Africans internally and socially. Let's call these two expressions of salvation, personal sanctification and social sanctification. J. Deotis Roberts states,

"There is much 'Spirit talk' today. Many questions are being asked about this cardinal doctrine of the Christian faith. Recently, I received a letter asking: 'Why are not liberation theologians writing about the Holy Spirit? Is there no Spirit talk among the Liberation theologians, black feminists, or Latin Americans?'" (Roberts 1987, 53).

In Luke 4:18-21, Jesus quotes Isaiah 61 saying that the Spirit of the Lord God was anointing Him to proclaim liberty to the captives and to set at liberty those who are oppressed. So how can anyone wanting God to liberate them and use them to liberate others neglect the Holy Spirit of liberation? If indeed James Cone and others believe the civil rights movement was a Spirit movement, then how did they not develop and discuss the quintessential importance of the Holy Spirit? If the language of God is left out, it is no wonder many do not view the Civil Rights Movement as a God thing. Promoting civil rights without the spiritual language sounds secular. A stronger case for including social transformation in the redemptive work of God would be to place it in the proper theological context of sanctification.

In other words, if salvation is just spiritual or heavenly and not social, the African remains in the present state of social death. The justification of the sinner comes only as a result of the Holy Spirit convincing us of the Savior's work. One can become a believer while still being prejudice, but under the work of sanctification, the Holy Spirit cleanses all believers of their sinful ways. The work of sanctification is both simultaneous and progressive. It would be more appropriate to consider that we all come to Christ as we are, and He changes us over a lifetime to be more like Him. Salvation comes from trusting in the finished work of Christ on the cross. Black theologians are right, that the Gospel should change you to the point that you care about and become actively engaged in the plight of the oppressed. This understanding of caring about the oppressed is called incarnational ministry. In the atonement, Christ acts as the cosmic redeemer and social redeemer. The new Heaven and new earth is also a new social order. The

White church has failed at understanding the full implications of redemption.

The Gospel can cure even the sin of racial prejudice and racism. Scholars have shown that the Word of God is replete with explicit texts and the Church does not have to stretch the Scriptures to find texts to address this problem. Paul the apostle, a Jew of the tribe of Benjamin, was called by God to be an apostle to the Gentiles. He was born at a key time in history when the world was filled with racial hostility. The book of Acts highlights the measure of suffering Paul went through in obeying the Lord, as a Jew ministering to Gentiles. There was ongoing hostility between the two ethnicities and Paul's suffering came from both sides for the same reason: racial prejudice. Paul was a peacemaker and he paid the price for trying to bring unity.

In Ephesians 2, Paul says that the Jews, as well as the rest of the world were suffering from racial enmity. The Jews in particular understood the hostility, yet walked in religious pride knowing they were the Israel of

God. Their view was that when Messiah comes, He would destroy their enemies. God had another plan; His plan was to bring Jew and Gentile together as one. Paul received a vision from God of the one new man (Ephesians 2:15). As a result of the vision, he would not allow hostility or hatred from his own ethnicity or Gentile nations to sway him from the will of God. He was persuaded to preach the Gospel to all and teach racial reconciliation with great conviction and joy.

Paul conveys that Christ is not only Israel's redeemer, but also the redeemer of all humankind. Jesus, by shedding His blood, had washed away the hostility between all humans regardless of nationality, gender, or social status. In Ephesians 2:14, the barrier that was removed speaks of the temple in Jerusalem and the walls it had between the different categories of people. There were the priests, the men of Israel, then the women, and finally the Gentiles. This does not mean that there are no differences between genders and nationalities, but rather that we should not be prejudiced because of our differences. We now have a common Savior, who at the shedding of His blood becomes our peace.

The salvation offered through Jesus reveals the heart of God for humankind. He wants all people to reach out to each other and love one another as one family in Christ. This is the purpose of the Father, that all His children recognize each other as equal in worth in the sight of their Creator. Through Christ, we can become like the triune God. God wants to create one family. Redemption is the good news for racism. Paul clearly states that the Gospel must be proclaimed to all humankind. We need to follow Paul as he followed Christ. Pauline theology is replete with a salvation/race reconciliation concept. Today, we live in a nation with the same racial problems as the ancient world had in Paul's day. We need to put into action the ministry of reconciliation (2 Corinthians 5:18), and preach the Gospel in America. If God is committed to reconciliation, the Church in America must have the same agenda. We need a redemptive dialogue by the Word and Spirit of God. All must endure the suffering that comes from executing the mission of the Church in this life, to be salt and light as our Lord commands us, giving all the opportunity to be saved and delivered to love as they should, regardless of the racial hostility demonstrated towards them.

In the end, Paul will enter eternity having fought a good fight. This should be our goal as well. We should form coalitions between the Black and White churches on this issue as part of the great commission and the great commandment. We need to preach to all and love each other, so the world may believe Jesus came to this world to save.

According to the Word of God, we are judicially one in Christ. We now need to enter into this truth experientially. Ephesians 3:14-16, tells us that by prayer we can be strengthened by the Holy Spirit to love, forgive, and reconcile as we (believers) ought. It is a supernatural act of God; that is why there is no excuse for Christians. Only those who are praying and allowing God to change their hearts are open to talk to each other. Another skill needed is called our *plausibility structure*. We must hear each other and remain civil, which lends itself to a redemptive dialogue.

CHAPTER FOUR

DIVINE DRAMA ACT 4:
DOCTRINE OF CONSUMMATION

Where Do We Go from Here?

The complete Gospel story contains the four divine acts of creation, fall, redemption, and consummation. Consummation answers the philosophical question of what happens after death or where do we go from here? In the consummation of all things, we see the final scene of human history before the Lord comes. In Revelation 7:9, John the Revelator is caught up into Heaven and sees history unfolding from the perspective of God's throne. John says that when Jesus opened the book, he saw all of humanity represented around the throne, a great multitude of all nations, tribes, peoples and tongues.

In John 14:1-6, Jesus comforts the disciples by instructing them why He had to leave and what He would be doing. Heaven is a place where evil is totally destroyed; no more pain, suffering, death, fallen human nature, or racial hostility. This is a vision that should motivate all Christians to fight the good fight of faith. We will all be in Heaven together and it will have been worth it all. For we are citizens of another kingdom and this world is not our home. He is preparing a place for us all, and where He is, we can be also. The goal of a Christian is to see Him face to face. The eternal bliss of Heaven is called glorification. We will spend eternity without the fallen sin-nature anymore; we shall possess incorporeal bodies. We will be in eternal fellowship with the divine council of Heaven as well as the divine council on earth.

Consummation and Racism

The Bible teaches that God will bring this world to an end. He will make a new Heaven and a new earth. All racism and prejudice will come to an end. There will be no wall of separation between the Black and White churches. Jesus said He had come from Heaven and was returning to Heaven. He promised to also come from Heaven at the end of the age, to receive the Church unto Himself (John 14:3).

Here we have the truth conveyed that people from all ages, ethnicities, and languages will fill Heaven around God's throne, for His glory and pleasure. The end resolution is for the Church to please her Lord and accomplish His good pleasure. How hard would it be for people who hate each other to together rejoice with their Lord, who loves all His children? He wants to bring His family together for eternity.

We should keep this vision before us and labor with the heart of God in mind. After all, He gave His life for us all to be one with each other, and one with Him. This is the ultimate quest for the Christian; to please God by loving one another as God loves us. We should want to see the pleasure on His face as He sits on the throne with all His children around Him.

SUMMARY

In summary, what I have tried to establish is that God is the author of the whole human race. He alone decided that variety among humans is a good thing. Not only did He create all ethnicities, He also orchestrated interracial marriages and relations to facilitate His divine plan for Israel and the Gentiles. Throughout Scripture, God brings about His purposes without prejudice toward people, yet He differentiates based on the worship of false gods. Therefore, the concept of false gods is the only place where God discriminates. God was laying the groundwork for the mystery of the one new man, found in the book of Ephesians. Heaven will be populated with all kinds of people and that will please the heart of God.

We have analyzed the impact of racism on the Gospel. Worldly philosophies, Augustine's theological framework of sacred realms versus secular realms, racism in White theology and Darwinian evolution have been overwhelming influences on the Gospel. Their impact on eternity is something only God can measure.

The first and second Great Awakenings were the move of God to bring Blacks into the kingdom of God and eventually move this nation toward racial equality. The Civil War erupted and became a major act of God's judgment against American racism. President Abraham Lincoln mentioned this possible judgment in his second inaugural address. Then, the reconstruction period was initially a bright spot in American history. Had reconstruction continued, it could have been a great transition period to bring healing to this nation. However, it was pushed back by the reassertion of white supremacy through Jim Crowism and black codes, among other issues. The withdrawal of federal troops by President Rutherford Hayes was the impetus for the nation's digression.

The birth of the Black church is a direct reaction to the worldview of white supremacy demonstrated by White churches toward the Blacks. The Black church is the vital key to the survival and development of the Black community and its role in American culture. There was a reaction to the national disposition towards black betterment, which led to the black power movement. This is part of the reason Black theology, or liberation theology developed under the leadership of James Cone. This theology is in partial error from orthodox theology, yet it is a challenge to compete with the Eurocentric emphasis of the Western church, which also has partially deviated from orthodox theology.

We have looked at several components that contributed to the wall of separation between the Black church and White church of America. The wall of separation went up long before the Europeans decided to come to America. The moment the Europeans decided to justify slavery with many unsubstantiated assumptions in their theological heresy, the wall went up. The great cover-up was the glue that held the wall together.

DR. VAN B GAYTON

There is such a great need for the Black church and White church to study the history that led to the wall of separation. This must be done all with a proper understanding of the Gospel creation, fall, redemption, and consummation. Only those who know history make history. Our younger generations need this education, or we will continue to perpetuate the myth of white superiority over Blacks. This distortion keeps our whole nation from reaching its potential. God can heal the rift. The whole Church beginning with its leadership, can lead our nation into the knowledge of God. The one new man concept that the Apostle Paul taught in Ephesians can only be demonstrated by cooperating with the Holy Spirit.

The Scripture says that if you say you love God but hate your brother, you are still in darkness (1 John 2:9). Our greatest need is to have our hearts transformed, to have Christ take out the evil in us and put in a heart of holiness and love. Blessed are the pure in heart, for they shall see as God sees (Matthew 5:8). In God's economy, He sees His Son reflected in us all. How can we say we love God and hate our brother? Only God can give us a clean, loving heart toward Him and others. If we are truly of God, He will empower us to fulfill His purposes relationally. At the cross, He has destroyed the hatred and strife between the races; a message not often preached or taught enough in the Church. We should not skip over this subject when our nation is riddled with hatred and animosity. The Church is meant to lead with a ministry of reconciliation.

The process will not be instantaneous, for sanctification is a lifelong journey. When we as Christians speak of change from human to divine, this is called sanctification. In other words, you can be justified, but sanctification is progressive. I am saved, I am being saved, and I shall be saved. The theological terms are justification, sanctification, and glorification. If all of us need to be sanctified, and we do, then a full, daily surrender to the work of the cross will deliver us all. When we look at Calvary, how can we not love each other for His sake? If one has truly come to faith, or as some describe it, is saved, then one becomes a new creation. Jesus lived, died, and rose again to restore humankind back to God and to each other. This He did because He loves His creation. The *missio Dei* (mission of God) is accomplished now through the Church by the power of the Holy Spirit. The born-again experience is essential to becoming a Christian. Yes, we are to confess and believe, but without the Holy Spirit, one cannot really confess Christ and truly believe unto salvation. The Holy Spirit convicts us of sin, with righteous judgment. Without the Holy Spirit, we only have intellectual or emotional conversion. This is a factor of truth that is either missing or not pronounced enough in the Church today.

This book is meant to be heuristic, meaning that it raises issues that require ongoing dialogue. The subject matter is too much and too diverse to cover in one setting. Despite the seemingly insurmountable obstacles, our hope is in the power of the Good News, for it will liberate us and reconcile us to Christ. Shalom to all my Black and White brothers and sisters.

Anyike, James. *Historical Christianity African Centered.* Chicago: Winston-Derek Publishers Group, Inc., 1995.

Augustine of Hippo, Saint. *The City of God.* Trans. Marcus Dods. New York: Random House, 1950.

Barclay, William. *The Letters to the Galatians and Ephesians.* Philadelphia: The Westminster Press, 1976.

Barndt, Joseph. *Dismantling Racism: The Continuing Challenge to White America.* Minneapolis, MN: Augsburg Fortress, 1991.

Cone, James H. *For My People: Black Theology and the Black Church.* 4th printing. Maryknoll, NY: Orbis Books, 1984.

Douglass, Frederick. *Life & Times of Frederick Douglass.* Secaucus, NJ: Citadel Press, 1983.

Du Bois, W.E.B. *The Souls of Black Folks.* New York: Barnes & Noble Books, 2003.

Ellis, Carl. *Free at Last? The Gospel in the African-American Experience.* Downers Grove, IL: Inter- Varsity Press, 1996.

Epstein, I. (ed.), Jacob Shachater, and H. Freedman (trans.). *Tractate Sanhedrin: Hebrew-English Edition of the Babylonian Talmud*. London: Soncino Press Ltd., 1969.

Felder, Cain Hope. *The Original African Study Bible*. Iowa Fall, IA: World Bible Publishers, Inc., 1993.

Gerbner, Katharine. *Christian Slavery: Conversion and Race in the Protestant Atlantic World*. Philadelphia, PA: Penn Press, 2018.

Ham, K., and A.C. Ware. *Darwin's Plantation: Evolution's Racist Roots*. Green Forest, AR: Master Books, 2007.

Ham, K., and A.C. Ware. *One Race One Blood: A Biblical Answer to Racism*. Green Forest, AR: Master Books, 2010.

Hodge, Charles. "The Fugitive Slave Act." In *Cotton is King, and Pro-Slavery Arguments*. Edited by E.N. Elliott, 815-816. Augusta, GA: Pritchard, Abbott & Loomis, 1860.

Isaac, Benjamin. *The Invention of Racism in Classical Antiquity*. Princeton: NJ: Princeton University Press, 2004.

Jones, William R. *Is God a White Racist? A Preamble to Black Theology*. Boston: Beacon Press, 1997.

King, Martin Luther Jr. "Remaining Awake Through a Great Revolution," delivered at the National Cathedral, Washington, D.C., on 31 March 1968 and written in the *Congressional Record*, on 9 April 1968.

Lincoln, Abraham. "Second Inaugural Address of Abraham Lincoln." *The Avalon Project: Documents in Law, History, and Diplomacy*. http://avalon.law.yale.edu /19thcentury/lincoln2.asp (accessed on 15 March 2014).

Lincoln, C. Eric, and Lawrence H. Mamiya. *The Black Church in the African American Experience*. 3rd Impression. Durham, NC: Duke University Press, 1990.

Moyd, Olin P. *Redemption in Black Theology*. 2nd printing. Valley Forge, PA: Judson Press, 1997.

Moyers, Bill. *Bill Moyers Journal*. James Cone Interview, 23 November 2007, PBS Network transcript. http:// www.pbs.org/moyers/journal/11232007/transcript1.html (accessed 14 December 2013).

Noll, Mark A. *The Scandal of the Evangelical Mind*. Grand Rapids, MI: Eerdmans Publishing Co., 1994.

Noll, Mark A. America's God: From Jonathan Edwards to Abraham Lincoln. New York: Oxford University Press Inc., 2002.

Oden, Thomas C. *How Africa Shaped the Christian Mind: Rediscovering the African Seedbed of Western Christianity*. Downers Grove, IL: InterVarsity Press, 2007.

Roberts, J. Deotis. *Black Theology in Dialogue.* Philadelphia, PA: Westminster John Knox Press, 1987.

Robinson, Randall. *The Debt: What America Owes to Blacks.* New York: Dutton, 2000.

Rosser, R.C. "A Multiethnic Model of the Church." *Ministry Compass.* Vol. 27, No. 2 (Fall 1998): 189-192.

Shelton, Jason E., and Michael O. Emerson. *Blacks and Whites in Christian America: How Racial Discrimination Shapes Religious Convictions.* New York: New York University Press, 2012.

Sherman, William T. "General Sherman Enacts 'Forty Acres and a Mule'". *African American Registry 1865.* https://aaregistry.org/story/general-sherman-enacts-forty-acres-and-a-mule/ (accessed on 12 May 2014).

Sproul, R.C. "Defending Your Faith: An Overview of Classical Apologetics," *Ligonier Ministries.* DVD Teaching Series, 2001.

Warnock, Raphael G. *The Divided Mind of the Black Church: Theology, Piety, & Public Witness.* New York: New York University Press, 2013.

Webb, William J. "A Redemptive-Movement Hermeneutic The Slavery Analogy." In *Discovering Biblical Equality Complementarity Without Hierarchy.* Edited by Ronald W. Pierce, Rebecca M. Groothuis, and Gordon D. Fee, 382-400. Downers Grove, IL: InterVarsity Press, 2005.

Williams, Chancellor. *The Destruction of Black Civilization: Great Issues of a Race From 4500 B.C. to 2000 A.D.* Chicago, IL: Third World Press, 1987. Quoted in Joel A. Freeman and Don B. Griffin, *Return to Glory: The Powerful Stirring of the Black Race.* [Shippensburg, PA: Treasure House Publishers, 2003].

.

Printed in Great Britain
by Amazon

72505914R00076